NEXT-GEN GOSPEL

No part of this book may be reproduced, stored in retrieval system, or transmitted in any form whatsoever, without the publisher's permission in writing.

Eric King © 2019
ISBN 978-1-9990646-2-4
Almighty Books

John 1

¹ In the beginning was the Word, and the Word was with God, and the Word is God. ² He existed with God in the beginning. ³ All things were made through him, and nothing was made without him. ⁴ Life was in him, and that life was imparted as the light of men. ⁵ The light shines in the darkness, and the darkness did not prevail.

⁶ God sent a man named John, ⁷ and he came as a witness to proclaim about the light, so that all would hear and believe. ⁸ John was not the light; he was simply a messenger of the light. ⁹ The true light that spreads light to everyone was coming into the world.

¹⁰ He was in the world that he created, and the world did not know him. ¹¹ He came unto his own people, and they did not receive him. ¹² But to all who welcomed him, and to those who believed in him, he gave them the right to become the children of God: ¹³ they were not born by blood, or by the will of flesh, or by the will of man, but they were born of God. ¹⁴ The Word became flesh and dwelt among us, and we observed his glory, the glory of the Father's only begotten Son, full of grace and truth.

¹⁵ John testified about him and exclaimed, "This is the one I was talking about when I said, 'Someone coming after me is greater than I am,' because he existed before me." ¹⁶ From the fullness of God, we have all received grace after grace. ¹⁷ For the law was given through Moses,

grace and truth came into being through Jesus Christ. ¹⁸ No one has ever seen God except the only begotten Son who is near to the Father's heart, has made God known.

¹⁹ Now this was John's testimony when the Jewish leaders from Jerusalem sent priests and Levites to ask him who he was. ²⁰ He did not refuse to answer, but he declared, "I am not the messiah." ²¹ And they asked him, "Well who are you? Are you Elijah?" He said, "No, I am not." "Are you the prophet?" "The answer is no." ²² "Then who are you, really? We have to give an answer to those who sent us."

²³ John said, "I am the voice of one calling out in the wilderness, 'prepare the way for the Lord's coming,' as the prophet Isaiah had said." ²⁴ Those sent by the Pharisees ²⁵ asked him, "If you are not the Messiah, or Elijah, or the Prophet, then why do you baptize?" ²⁶ John said, "I baptize with water, and you don't know the person who stands among you." ²⁷ He is the one who comes after me, and I am unworthy to untie his sandal straps. ²⁸ This all happened at Bethany across the Jordan, where John was baptizing.

²⁹ The next day John saw Jesus coming toward him and he said, "This is the lamb of God, who takes away the sin of the world!" ³⁰ This is the one I meant when I said, "He who comes af-

ter me is greater than I am because he existed before me." ³¹ I did not recognize him, but I have been baptizing with water so that he would be revealed to Israel."

³² John testified, "I saw the Spirit descend from heaven like a dove and rest upon him. ³³ I did not know him, but the one who sent me to baptize with water told me, 'The one you see the Spirit descend and rest upon, is the one who baptizes with the Holy Spirit.' ³⁴ I have seen and testified that this is the Son of God." ³⁵ The next day John stood there again with two of his disciples. ³⁶ When he saw Jesus passing by, he said, "Behold, the Lamb of God!"

³⁷ The two disciples heard this and followed Jesus at once. ³⁸ Jesus turned around and saw them following. He said, "What are you searching for?" They answered, "Rabbi (which means teacher), where are you staying?" ³⁹ He said, "Come and see." They went to the place where he was staying, and they remained with him rest of the day: for it was about the tenth hour. ⁴⁰ Andrew, Simon Peter's brother, was one of the two disciples who heard what John said and followed Jesus. ⁴¹ First he went to find his brother Simon to tell him the news, "We found the Messiah," (which means Christ,) ⁴² and he brought him to Jesus. Jesus saw him and said, "You are Simon

the son of John, and you will be called Cephas" (which means Peter).

⁴³ The next day Jesus decided to leave for Galilee, and he found Philip. He said, "Come, follow me." ⁴⁴ Philip came from Bethsaida, the hometown of Andrew and Peter. ⁴⁵ Philip found Nathanael and told him the news, "We found the one that Moses wrote about in the Law, the same person that the Prophets wrote about. It's Jesus of Nazareth, the son of Joseph!" ⁴⁶ Nathanael said, "Can anything good come from Nazareth?" And Philip said, "Come and see."

⁴⁷ Jesus saw Nathanael coming towards him and said of him, "Here is a true Israelite in whom there is no deceit." ⁴⁸ Nathanael said, "How do you know me?" Jesus replied, "I saw you under the fig tree before Philip called you." ⁴⁹ Then Nathanael said, "Rabbi, you are the Son of God, the king of Israel." ⁵⁰ Jesus said, "Do you believe because I told you that I saw you under the fig tree? You will see greater things than this." ⁵¹ Then he said, "Truly and certainly, you will see heaven open and the angels of God descending and ascending on the Son of Man."

John 2

¹ A wedding was held on the third day in Cana of Galilee, and the mother of Jesus was there. ² Jesus and his disciples were also guests at the wedding. ³ When the wine ran out, Jesus' mother said to him, "They are out of wine." ⁴ Jesus said, "Woman, what does this have to do with me? My time has not yet come." ⁵ His mother said to the servants, "Do whatever he tells you to do."

⁶ Standing nearby were six stone water jars for Jewish purification, containing twenty or thirty gallons each. ⁷ Jesus told the servants, "Fill the jars with water," and they filled them to the brim. ⁸ Then he instructed them, "Now draw some out and take it to the master of ceremonies." They did as they were told.

⁹ The master of ceremonies tasted the water that was now wine, not knowing where it came from, but the servants that drew the water knew. He called the groom and said, ¹⁰ "Everyone serves the best wine first, before bringing out the lower-grade wine when the guests had a lot to drink. But you have kept the best wine until now." ¹¹ This was the first miracle of Jesus in Cana of Galilee that displayed his glory, and his disciples believed in him.

¹² After the wedding he went to Capernaum with his mother, his brothers, and his disciples for a few days. ¹³ Jesus went up to Jerusalem

when it was almost time for the Jewish Passover. ¹⁴ He saw vendors selling cattle, sheep, and doves, and the currency traders seated at tables within the temple zone. ¹⁵ He made a whip out of cords, and drove them all out of the temple yard with their animals. Then he swiped off the coins and flipped the tables of the money traders.

¹⁶ He marched over to the dove sellers and said, "Get these out of here, and stop turning my Father's house into a market!" ¹⁷ In that moment, his disciples remembered that it was written, "Zeal for your house will consume me." ¹⁸ The Jewish leaders responded to him, "By what right do you have to do all this? Show us a miraculous sign to prove your authority?"

¹⁹ Jesus said, "Destroy this temple, and in three days I will raise it up." ²⁰ They replied, "It took forty-six years to construct this temple, and you think you can rebuild it in three days? ²¹ But the temple that he referred to was his body. ²² After he was raised from the dead, the disciples remembered his words, and they believed the scripture and the words that Jesus said. ²³ Many at the Passover Festival began to trust in his name because they saw his miracles. ²⁴ But Jesus wouldn't trust them, because he knew them all. ²⁵ No one needed to tell him about human nature, for he knew what was in people's hearts.

John 3

¹ Now there was a Jewish leader named Nicodemus, and he was a Pharisee. ² He went to Jesus at night and said, "Rabbi, we know you are a teacher from God, for the miracles that you made cannot be done without him. ³ Jesus replied, "Truly I say to you, unless you are born again, you cannot see the kingdom of God." ⁴ Nicodemus said, "How can a man to be born when he is old? Can he go back into his mother's womb and be born again?"

⁵ Jesus answered, "Truly I say to you, unless you are born of water and the Spirit, you cannot enter the kingdom of God. ⁶ What is born of the flesh is flesh, and what is born of the Spirit is spirit. ⁷ Do not be surprised that I said, 'You must be born again.' ⁸ The wind blows where it wants to go, and you hear its sound, but cannot tell where it comes from or where it is going. You cannot explain how people are born of the Spirit." ⁹ Nicodemus said, "How are these things possible?"

¹⁰ Jesus replied, "You are Israel's teacher, and you do not understand these things? ¹¹ Truly and certainly, we speak what we know and have seen, and you don't accept our testimony. ¹² If you don't believe when I speak of earthly things, then how would you believe when I speak of heavenly matters? ¹³ No one has gone up into heaven and returned, except the Son of Man who came from

heaven. ⁱ⁴ For the reason that Moses lifted the snake in the wilderness, so must the Son of Man be lifted up, ¹⁵ so that everyone who believes in him will get eternal life.

¹⁶ For God so loved the world that he gave his one true Son, that whoever believes in him will not perish but have eternal life. ¹⁷ For God did not send his Son into the world to judge it, but to save the world through him. ¹⁸ Whoever believes in him isn't judged, but anyone who does not believe is judged already for not believing in God's one true son.

¹⁹ And the judgment is that light entered the world, and people loved darkness instead of light because their deeds were wicked. ²⁰ Everyone who does evil hates the light and will not enter into it, so that their sins won't be exposed. ²¹ But whoever lives by truth comes into the light, to make evident that his works are done in accordance with God."

²² Afterwards, Jesus and his disciples went into the Judean countryside, where he spent some time with them and baptized. ²³ John was also baptizing in Aenon near Salim, because there was so much water there and people came to be baptized, ²⁴ since John was not put into prison as of yet.

²⁵ Then a disagreement arose between

John 3

John's disciples and a certain Jew over ceremonial cleansing. ²⁶ They came to John and said, "Rabbi, the man who was with you across the Jordan, the one you testified about, is baptizing and everyone is going to him."

²⁷ John responded, "No one can receive anything unless it is given to him from heaven. ²⁸ You yourselves know that I said, 'I am not the Messiah, for I have been sent ahead of him.' ²⁹ The groom is the one who marries the bride, and the best man who stands by, is filled with joy when he hears the groom speak. This joy of mine is now complete.

³⁰ He must become greater, while I become less. ³¹ He who comes from above is greater than all, while those from the world belongs to the world and speaks of worldly matters, but he who came from heaven is greater than all.

³² He testifies to what he has seen and heard yet no one believes his testimony. ³³ Whoever receives his witness affirms that God is true, ³⁴ and the one sent by God speaks God's words, for he was given the Spirit without measure. ³⁵ The Father loves the Son and has passed everything into his hands. ³⁶ Those who believe in the Son has eternal life, but those who reject the Son will not see life, for the wrath of God remains on him."

John 4

¹ Jesus knew that the Pharisees heard he was gaining and baptizing more disciples than John, ² although it was not him that baptized, but his disciples were. ³ So he left Judea to return to Galilee, ⁴ and Samaria was on the route. ⁵ He came to a town in Samaria called Sychar, and it was near the field that Jacob gave to his son Joseph. ⁶ Jacob's well was there, and Jesus tired from the journey, sat down beside the well when it was about noon.

⁷ A Samaritan woman came to draw water, and Jesus said, "Give me a drink." ⁸ His disciples had gone away into the town to buy some food. ⁹ She said, "You are a Jew and you are asking me, a Samaritan woman for a drink?" ¹⁰ Jesus answered, "If you knew the gift that God has for you and who you speak to, you would ask me and I would give you living water." ¹¹ The woman said, "But sir, you don't have a rope or a bucket and this well is very deep. Where would you get this living water? ¹² How can you be greater than our ancestor Jacob, who gave us this well and drank from it, as did his sons and animals?" ¹³ Jesus replied, "Anyone who drinks this water will soon become thirsty again, ¹⁴ but those who drink the water that I give would not thirst anymore. It becomes a fresh spring of water that rises up within them, giving eternal life."

John 4

¹⁵ The woman said, "Give me this water so I won't be thirsty again and I won't have to return to get water." ¹⁶ Then Jesus said, "Go, bring your husband here." ¹⁷ The woman replied, "I don't have a husband," and Jesus said, "You are right when you said you have no husband; ¹⁸ you had five husbands, and you are not married to the man you are living with now." ¹⁹ The woman said, "Sir, you must be a prophet, ²⁰ so why is it that you Jews insist that Jerusalem is the only place of worship, while we Samaritans claim it is here at Mount Gerizim, where our ancestors worshipped?"

²¹ Jesus answered, "Believe me dear woman, the time is coming when it will not matter whether you worship God on this mountain or in Jerusalem. ²² You Samaritans do not know about the God you worship, but we Jews know him, for salvation comes through the Jews. ²³ The time is coming and it is here when true believers will worship God in spirit and in truth. He is searching for those who will worship him that way. ²⁴ For the Father is Spirit, and those who believe in him must worship in spirit and truth." ²⁵ The woman said, "I know the Messiah is coming, the one we call Christ, and he will explain everything to us when he comes." ²⁶ Jesus declared, "I am the one you call Christ."

⁲⁷ His disciples returned on the spot, surprised to find him talking with a woman. They dared not ask, "What do you want with her?" or "Why are you speaking with her?" ²⁸ The woman left her water jar behind, and hurried back to town and said to everyone, ²⁹ "Come and see a man who told me everything I ever did. Can he be the Messiah?" ³⁰ Then people came flooding from town to see Christ. ³¹ For now, his disciples urged him, "Rabbi, eat something." ³² But he replied, "I have something to eat that you don't know about." ³³ The disciples said to each other, "Did someone bring him food while we were gone?"

³⁴ Jesus explained, "My nourishment comes from doing the will of God, who sent me, and to finish his work. ³⁵ You know the saying, 'Four months of planting remains until the harvest.' But I say, wake up and see that the fields are ripe for harvest. ³⁶ The workers are paid good wages, and they gather a fruit that is people brought to eternal life, so the planters and harvesters may rejoice together. ³⁷ You know the saying is true, 'One plants and another harvests.' ³⁸ I sent to you harvest where you did not plant; others have done the work, and you get to gather the harvest."

³⁹ Many Samaritans from that town believed in him because the woman had said, "He

John 4

told me everything I ever did." ⁴⁰ When they came to see him, they asked him to stick around, and he stayed with them for two days. ⁴¹ Many more of them heard his message and believed in him. ⁴² They said to the woman, "We no longer believe because of what you said, for we have heard for ourselves and know that this is truly the Savior of the world."

⁴³ Jesus departed for Galilee after two days, ⁴⁴ and he did say that a prophet is not honoured in his own nation. ⁴⁵ Despite his words, the Galileans welcomed him, for they had seen everything that he did in Jerusalem during the Passover festival. ⁴⁶ He returned to Cana in Galilee, where he had transformed water into wine. And there was a royal official whose son was sick at Capernaum. ⁴⁷ When he heard that Jesus came from Judea into Galilee, he went to plead with him to come and heal his son, who was about to die.

⁴⁸ Jesus told him, "You won't have faith unless you see a miracle." ⁴⁹ The official pleaded, "Come with me before my son dies," ⁵⁰ and Jesus said, "Go home, your son will live." The man believed what Jesus said, and he departed. ⁵¹ While the man was on the way, his servants met him and said that his son was alive. ⁵² He asked what time the son got better and they told him, "The fever departed yesterday at the seventh hour." ⁵³

Then the father realized that this was the same time when Jesus said, "Your son will live." He and his entire household believed in in Jesus. ⁵⁴ This was the second miracle that Jesus made after coming from Judea into Galilee.

John 5

¹ Afterward, Jesus went to Jerusalem for one of the Jewish festivals. ² Inside the city near the sheep gate was a pool called Bethesda, which was covered by five porches. ³ Crowds of the sick, blind, lame, or paralyzed individuals waited for the water to move. ⁴ This was due to an angel descending into the pool at a particular season to stir the water. Whoever entered the pool immediately after the water was stirred would recover from any sickness.

⁵ One of the men that were present was sick for thirty-eight years. ⁶ When Jesus saw him lying there and knew that he was sick for a long time, he asked, "Do you want to get better?" ⁷ The sick man answered, "I have no one to put me into the pool when it is stirred, and when I try to get in, someone gets there first." ⁸ Jesus said, "Get up, pick up your mat and walk." ⁹ The man recovered at once, and he picked up his mat and walked. This happened on the Sabbath.

¹⁰ For that reason, the Jewish leaders told the man that Jesus healed, "It is the Sabbath, and the law forbids you to carry your mat." ¹¹ But he replied, "The man who made me well told me, 'Pick up your mat and walk.' " ¹² They asked, "Who is the man that told you to pick up your mat and walk." ¹³ The man that was cured did not know who healed him, for Jesus had vanished

into the crowd. ⁱ⁴ Eventually, Jesus found him in the temple and said, "Know that you are well, and be careful not to sin, or something worse may happen to you." ¹⁵ The man went to report to the Jewish leaders that it was Jesus who healed him. ¹⁶ So the Jews began to persecute Jesus for doing these things on the Sabbath. ¹⁷ Jesus said, "My Father is always working, and so am I." ¹⁸ This made the Jews more determined to kill him: For he was breaking the Sabbath, claiming to be God's son, and making himself equal with God.

¹⁹ Jesus said, "Truly I say to you, the Son can do nothing by himself. He does only what he sees the Father doing. What the Father does, the Son does also. ²⁰ For the Father loves the Son and shows him everything that he does. The Father will show him greater works than these, so that you will be amazed. ²¹ As the Father raises the dead and gives them life, the Son also gives life to whomever he selects. ²² The Father does not judge at all, for he has entrusted all judgment to the Son, ²³ that everyone would honour the Son as they honour the Father. Anyone who does not honour the Son does not honour the Father who sent him. ²⁴ Truly and certainly, whoever hears my word and believes in the one who sent me has eternal life and will not fall under judgment but has passed from death to life. ²⁵ Truly and

John 5

certainly, the hour is coming, and it is here now, when the dead will hear the voice of God's Son, and those who hear it will live. ²⁶ For as the Father has life in himself, he has granted the Son to have life in himself. ²⁷ And he gave the Son the right to judge because he is the Son of Man. ²⁸ Do not be surprised, for a time is coming when all who are in their graves will hear his voice, ²⁹ and they will come out. Those who have done good will resurrect to eternal life, but those who did evil shall get the resurrection of judgment.

³⁰ I can do nothing on my own. I judge as I hear, and my judgment is just for it is not my will that I do, but the will of the one who sent me. ³¹ If I were to bear witness on my own behalf, my testimony would not be true, ³² but someone else testifies about me, and I know for certain that everything he says about me is true. ³³ You sent your people to John, and he testified to the truth. ³⁴ It is not that I don't need human witnesses, but I say these things so that you may be saved. ³⁵ John was a burning lamp that gave light, and for a time you were willing embrace his message, ³⁶ but I have a greater witness than John: I have my teachings and my miracles. These works that I have accomplished prove that the Father sent me, ³⁷ and the Father who sent me, has testified of me. You have not heard his voice, or seen his

form at any time. ⁳⁸ And you don't have his message dwelling in your hearts, because you don't believe in the one he sent.

³⁹ You search the scriptures believing that they give eternal life, while the scriptures refer to me, ⁴⁰ and you stubbornly refuse to come to me to receive life. ⁴¹ I can't accept glory from men, ⁴² because I am aware that you have no love for God within you. ⁴³ I came in my Father's name, and you have rejected me. Yet, you would gladly welcome others if they came in their own name.

⁴⁴ How can you believe, if you receive glory from one another, but do not seek the glory that comes from the one true God? ⁴⁵ I won't be the one to accuse you before the Father. Moses is your accuser, the one on whom you placed your hopes. ⁴⁶ If you believed Moses then you would believe in me, because he wrote of me. ⁴⁷ And if you don't believe his writings, then how would you believe what I say?"

John 6

¹ Eventually, Jesus crossed over the Sea of Galilee (or Tiberias). ² A great crowd followed him because they witnessed his miracles of healing the sick. ³ Jesus went up a mountain and sat with his disciples. ⁴ It was almost time for the Jewish Passover celebration. ⁵ Jesus saw the massive crowd that was coming towards him. He asked Philip, "Where can we buy bread to feed these people?" ⁶ He was testing Philip, for he knew what he intended to do. ⁷ Philip answered, "It would take more than six months wages to feed them one little bite."

⁸ Then the disciple Andrew, Simon Peter's brother, spoke of a small solution. ⁹ "There is a boy here with five barley loaves and two fish, but what could we do with so many people?" ¹⁰ Jesus said, "Tell everyone to sit down," and they all sat on the grassy plains. There were about five thousand men. ¹¹ Jesus took the loaves and gave thanks before distributing them to the people. The same was done with the fish and everyone had as much as they wanted. ¹² When they were full, he told his disciples, "Bring the leftovers so that nothing is wasted." ¹³ So they brought them, and filled twelve baskets with pieces from the five barley loaves left by those who had eaten. ¹⁴ When the people saw the miracle that he made, they said, "This certainly is the Prophet who was

coming into the world. ¹⁵ Jesus perceived that they would come and force him to be king, so he withdrew again to the mountain for solitary refuge.

¹⁶ That evening the disciples went down to the shoreline, ¹⁷ where they began to cross the sea by boat. They were headed for Capernaum, and Jesus had not returned by nightfall. ¹⁸ Soon a gale swept down on them, and the sea grew rough. ¹⁹ They had rowed three to four miles, and were terrified to see Jesus walking on water towards the boat. ²⁰ He called out to them, "It is I, don't be afraid." ²¹ Then they were willing to bring him on board, and immediately the boat arrived at their chosen destination.

²² The next day the crowd that stayed on the other side of the lake realized that the disciples took the only boat, and that Jesus had not departed with them. ²³ A few boats from Tiberias entered the place where they ate the bread after the Lord given thanks. ²⁴ So when the crowd saw that Jesus and his disciples weren't there, they took the boats to Capernaum in search of Jesus. ²⁵ They found him on the other side of lake and said, "Rabbi, when did you get here?" ²⁶ Jesus answered, "Truly I say to you, you seek me not because of the miracles that I made, but because you ate the bread and were filled. ²⁷ Don't labour

John 6

for the food that spoils, but do work for the food that leads to eternal life, which the Son of Man will give you. For God the Father has set his seal of approval on him."

²⁸ They asked, "What can we do to fulfill God's works?" ²⁹ Jesus answered, "God's work is for you to believe in the one he sent." ³⁰ They replied, "We need to see a miracle to believe in you. What can you show us? ³¹ Our ancestors ate the manna while they wandered in the wilderness, as it is written: he gave them bread from heaven to eat." ³² Jesus said, "Truly I say to you, Moses did not give you the bread from heaven, but my Father feeds you the real bread from heaven. ³³ The bread of God is the one who descends from heaven and gives life to the world." ³⁴ They said, "Sir, give us this bread every day."

³⁵ Jesus declared, "I am the bread of life. Whoever comes to me will never be hungry, and whoever believes in me will never be thirsty. ³⁶ But I said that you have seen me, and you do not believe. ³⁷ Everyone that is given to me by the Father will come to me, and I will not reject the people who turn to me. ³⁸ For I have descended from heaven to do God's will, instead of my own. ³⁹ And this is the will of God who sent me, that I should not lose anyone that he has given me, so that I could raise them up on the last day. ⁴⁰ My

Father's will is that everyone who sees the Son and believes in him should have eternal life, and I will raise them up on the last day."

⁴¹ Then the Jews grumbled about him because he said, "I am the bread that came down from heaven." ⁴² The people said, "Isn't this Jesus, the son of Joseph, whose father and mother we know? How can he say, 'I descended from heaven'?" ⁴³ Jesus rebutted, "Stop complaining among yourselves. ⁴⁴ Nobody can approach me unless the Father who sent me draws him to me, and I will resurrect him on the last day. ⁴⁵ It is written in the Prophets, 'God will teach everyone,' and everyone who hears the Father and learns from him comes to me. ⁴⁶ No one has seen the Father except the one who God sent. He has seen the Father. ⁴⁷ Truly and certainly, whoever believes has eternal life. ⁴⁸ I am the bread of eternal life. ⁴⁹ You're ancestors ate manna in the wilderness, and they are dead. ⁵⁰ This is the bread that came down from heaven so that anyone may eat of it and not die. ⁵¹ I am the living bread that came down from heaven. Anyone who eats this bread will live forever. The bread that I will give for the life of the world is my body." ⁵² The Jews argued about what he had said. "How can he give us his body to eat?"

⁵³ Again Jesus said, "Truly I say to you,

John 6

unless you eat the body of God's Son and drink his blood, you will not have the eternal life. ⁵⁴ I will raise anyone who eats my flesh and sips my blood to life on the last day. ⁵⁵ For my body is real food and my blood is real drink. ⁵⁶ Whoever eats my body and drinks my blood remains in me, and I in him. ⁵⁷ I live because of the living Father who sent me, and you will live because of me if you feed on me. ⁵⁸ I am the real bread that came down heaven. Your ancestors ate manna and died, but whoever eats this bread will live forever." ⁵⁹ He said those words while teaching in the synagogue in Capernaum.

⁶⁰ Many of his disciples said, "Who can accept such a difficult message?" ⁶¹ Jesus knew that his disciples were complaining on this matter, so he said to them, "Does this offend you? ⁶² Then what will you say if you see the Son of Man ascend to heaven again? ⁶³ The Spirit alone gives eternal life, and human effort achieves nothing. The words that I have spoken to you are spirit and life. ⁶⁴ But some of you do not believe." For Jesus had known at the start, who would not believe, and who would betray him. ⁶⁵ He told them, "This is why I said that nobody can come to me unless the Father permits him."

⁶⁶ Upon this, many of his disciples went away and deserted him. ⁶⁷ Jesus turned to the

twelve and said, "Will you be leaving then?" ⁶⁸ Simon Peter answered, "Lord, to whom can we go? You have the words of eternal life. ⁶⁹ We have come to faith and we believe you are the Holy one of God." ⁷⁰ Jesus said, "I chose the twelve of you, but one is a devil." ⁷¹ He was referring to Judas, Simon Iscariot's son, one of the twelve who would later betray him.

John 7

¹ After this, Jesus traveled in Galilee since he did not want to enter Judea, where the Jews were plotting his death. ² It was almost time for the Jewish festival of shelters, ³ and Jesus' brothers told him, "Leave this place and go to Judea, where your disciples can see your works. ⁴ Nobody works in secret when he seeks public recognition. If you do these works, then show yourself to the world." ⁵ Not one of his brothers believed in him. ⁶ Jesus replied, "My time has not come, but your time is always ready. ⁷ The world cannot hate you, but it does hate me because I accuse it of doing evil. ⁸ Go ahead to the festival. I won't be joining you there, because my time has not yet come."

⁹ After speaking those words, he stayed in Galilee. ¹⁰ His brothers went to the festival, then he went there in secret, while staying out of public view. ¹¹ The Jewish leaders were hunting for him at the festival, and they kept asking, "Where is he?" ¹² There was widespread whispering about him among the crowds at the festival. Some said, "He is a good man," and others said, "He is deceiving people." ¹³ Nonetheless, no one spoke publicly of him, for fear of the Jews.

¹⁴ Halfway through the festival, Jesus went up into the temple and began to teach. ¹⁵ The people were truly astonished and asked, "How did

he master the scriptures without being taught?" ¹⁶ Jesus answered, "My teaching is not my own, but comes from the one who sent me. ¹⁷ Whoever chooses to do God's will, will know if this teaching comes from God or if it is merely my own. ¹⁸ Those who speak for themselves wants glory only for themselves, but a person who seeks to honour the one who sent him speaks the truth, not lies. ¹⁹ Did Moses not give you the law? You have disregarded his commands, so why do you want to kill me?"

²⁰ The crowd said, "You have a demon. Who wants to kill you?" ²¹ Jesus replied, "I made one miracle and you were all amazed. ²² Moses gave you the law of circumcision, not that it comes from him, but it was passed on from the patriarchs, and you circumcise a man on the Sabbath. ²³ You circumcise a man on the Sabbath so that the Law of Moses is not broken, so why are you upset with me for healing a man on the Sabbath? ²⁴ Judge not by appearance, but judge correctly with the righteous judgment."

²⁵ Some of the people of Jerusalem said, "Is this not the man that they are trying to kill? ²⁶ Behold, he speaks openly and they have nothing to say to him. Do the leaders know he is the Messiah? ²⁷ But we know where this man is from. When the Messiah comes, no one will know

John 7

where he comes from."

²⁸ While Jesus was teaching in the Temple, he cried out, "You know me and you know where I come from. I'm not here on my own, but the one who sent me is true. You don't know him. ²⁹ But I know him because I came from him, and he has sent me." ³⁰ So they tried to seize him, but no one laid a hand on him because his time had not yet come. ³¹ Many in the crowd believed in him and said, "When the Messiah comes, will he do more miracles than this man has done?"

³² The Pharisees heard the crowd whispering these things about him, so the chief priests and Pharisees sent officers to arrest him. ³³ Jesus said, "I will be with you a little longer. Then I will return to the one who sent me. ³⁴ You will search for me but not find me, and you cannot go to where I am going." ³⁵ The Jews said to each other, "Where does he intend to go that we will not find him? Will he go to the Scattered among the Gentiles and teach the Greeks? ³⁶ What does he mean when he said, 'You will search for me but not find me, and you cannot go to where I am going'?"

³⁷ On the last and greatest day of the festival, Jesus stood up and shouted to the crowds, "If anyone is thirsty, let him come to me and drink. ³⁸ The one who believes in me, as the Scripture said, will have streams of living water flow from

his heart." ³⁹ He said this about the Spirit. The believers of Christ will receive the Spirit, for the Spirit was not given yet because Jesus was not yet glorified. ⁴⁰ After hearing those words, some of the people said, "This certainly is the Prophet." ⁴¹ Others said, "He is the Messiah." Still others said, "Will Christ appear from Galilee? ⁴² Does the Scripture not say that the Messiah comes from David's lineage and from the town of Bethlehem, where David was born?" ⁴³ So the crowd was divided about Jesus. ⁴⁴ Some of them hoped to arrest him, but no one laid a hand on him.

⁴⁵ Then the officers went to the high priests and Pharisees, who asked them, "Why haven't you brought him?" ⁴⁶ The police said, "No one has ever spoken like this." ⁴⁷ The Pharisees retorted, "Are you also being deceived? ⁴⁸ Did any of the rulers or Pharisees believe in him? ⁴⁹ But these people who don't know the law are cursed." ⁵⁰ Then Nicodemus, the leader who met Jesus on prior occasion, said, ⁵¹ "Does our law judge a man before it hears from him, and knows what he is doing?" ⁵² They replied, "Are you also from Galilee? Search the Scriptures, and you will know that a prophet does not emerge from Galilee." ⁵³ So they all went home.

John 8

¹ But Jesus returned to the Mount of Olives. ² He appeared in the temple at dawn, and everyone gathered around. So he sat down and began to teach them. ³ The scribes and Pharisees brought a woman caught in adultery, and made her stand in the center. ⁴ They said to Jesus, "Rabbi, this woman was caught in the act of adultery. ⁵ The Law of Moses says to stone this type of women. What do you say? ⁶ They said this to tempt him into giving them evidence to accuse him with.

Jesus bent down and wrote on the ground with his finger. ⁷ They persisted in asking him, he stood up and said, "Let him who is without sin, cast the first stone at home." ⁸ He bent down again and wrote on the ground. ⁹ Those who heard him departed one at a time, starting with the oldest, until only Jesus remained with the woman in the center. ¹⁰ Jesus stood up and said, "Woman, where are they? Did no one condemn you?" ¹¹ She answered, "No one, Lord." Jesus replied, "Neither do I. Go and sin no more."

¹² Jesus spoke to the people again and said, "I am the light of the world. Whoever follows me will never walk in darkness but shall have the light of life." ¹³ The Pharisees replied, "You speak about yourself. Your testimony is invalid."

¹⁴ Jesus replied, "Even if I speak about myself, my testimony is valid, since I know where

I came from and where I am going. You don't know where I come from or where I'm going. ¹⁵ You judge me by human standards, but I judge no one. ¹⁶ And if I judge, my judgment is true, because I am not alone. For the Father who sent me is with me. ¹⁷ It is written in your law, that the witness of two men is true. ¹⁸ I am one witness, and the Father who sent me is the other."

¹⁹ Then they asked, "Where is your father?" Jesus replied, "You don't know me or my Father. If you knew me, you would also know my Father." ²⁰ He said those words while he taught in the temple, and he was not arrested because it was not his time. ²¹ Jesus said to them again, "I am going away. You will search for me, but you will die in your sin. You cannot come to where I am going." ²² The Jews said, "Will he kill himself since he said we cannot go to where he is going?"

²³ Jesus told them, "You are from below, and I am from above. You belong to this world; I don't. ²⁴ I have said that you will die in your sins, and unless you believe that I am who I said I am, you will die in your sins." ²⁵ So they said, "Who are you?" Jesus answered, "I am who I said I was from the beginning. ²⁶ I have much judgment to pronounce on you, but the one who sent me is true, and what I have heard from him is what I say to the world."

John 8

⁲⁷ They did not understand that he was speaking about the Father. ²⁸ So Jesus said, "When you have lifted up the Son of Man's cross, then you will know that I am he. I do nothing on my own, but I say what the Father has taught me. ²⁹ The one who sent me is with me, and he has not deserted me, for I always do his will that pleases him." ³⁰ Then many who heard speak, came to faith. ³¹ So Jesus said to those who believed in him, "You certainly are my disciples if you stay faithful to my teachings. ³² And you will know the truth that will set you free." ³³ They said, "We are descendants of Abraham and have never been slaves, so how you say that we will be set free?"

³⁴ Jesus said, "Truly I say to you, everyone who sins is a slave to sin. ³⁵ The slave does not dwell in the house forever, but the son remains forever. ³⁶ So if the Son sets you free, you are free indeed. ³⁷ I know that you are Abraham's descendants, and some of you want to kill me because you have no room for my word. ³⁸ I speak of what I have seen in the Father's presence, and you do what you have heard from your father." ³⁹ They said, "Our father is Abraham." Jesus replied, "If you were Abraham's children, then you would follow his ways. ⁴⁰ But you are trying to kill me because I told you the truth, which I heard from God. This is unlike Abraham; he did no such thing.

But you are trying to kill me because of the truth, which I spoke and heard from God; Abraham did not do this. ⁴¹ You walk in the steps of your real father." They said, "We are legitimate children, and God is our one true Father."

⁴² Jesus replied, "If God were your Father, you would love me, because I came from God. I did not come on my own, but he sent me. ⁴³ Why can't you understand my words? It's because you are deaf towards me. ⁴⁴ You are the seeds of the devil, and you want to do your father's works. He was a murderer from the start and has never stood for the truth because there is no truth in him. When he lies, he speaks his native language, because he is a liar, and the father of lies. ⁴⁵ Now when I tell the truth, you truly don't believe me. ⁴⁶ Is anyone able to convict me of sin? And since I am telling the truth, why don't you believe me? ⁴⁷ Whoever belongs to God listens to his words. But you don't listen because you are not from God."

⁴⁸ The people replied, "Have we not said that you are a Samaritan possessed by a demon?" ⁴⁹ Jesus said, "I have no demon. But I honour the Father and you dishonour me. ⁵⁰ I don't seek my glory, but there is one who seeks it, and he is the judge. ⁵¹ Truly and certainly, whoever keeps my word will never see death."

⁵² The Jews said, "Now we know you have

John 8

a demon. Abraham is dead and so are the prophets, but you claim that whoever keeps your word will never die. ⁵³ Are you greater than our father Abraham? He is dead, and so are the prophets. Who do you think you are?"

⁵⁴ Jesus said, "The glory has no value if I seek it for myself. It is my Father who will glorify me, and you say that he is your God. ⁵⁵ You have never known him, but I know him, and if I said that I don't know him then I would be a liar like you. I know him, and I keep his word. ⁵⁶ Your father Abraham rejoiced to see the day of my coming. He saw it and was glad."

⁵⁷ The people said, "You are not near fifty years old. So how could say that you saw Abraham?" ⁵⁸ Jesus answered, "Truly I say to you, before Abraham was born, I am." ⁵⁹ At this time they picked up the stones to throw at him, but he hid himself and left the temple zone.

¹ As he passed by, he saw a man who was blind from birth. ² His disciples asked him, "Rabbi, whose sin caused this man to be born blind, was it him or his parents?" ³ Jesus answered, "It was not this man who sinned, or his parents, but it happened so the works of God could be seen in him. ⁴ We must complete the works of the one who sent me while there is daylight. Night is coming when no one can work. ⁵ When I remain in the world, I am the light of the world."

⁶ Then he spat on the ground, made mud with the saliva, and spread the mud on the man's eyes. ⁷ He told him, "Go wash yourself in the pool of Siloam" (Siloam means Sent). So the man went, washed, and came back seeing. ⁸ His neighbours and others who knew him as a beggar asked, "Isn't this the man who used to sit and beg?" ⁹ Some said, "It's him," while others said, "No, he resembles him." But the man insisted, "I am the same person." ¹⁰ So they asked him, "How did your eyes get healed?" ¹¹ He said, "The man they call Jesus made mud, spread it over my eyes, and told me to go in the pool of Siloam and wash. So I went and washed, and I received my sight." ¹² They asked, "Where is he now?" He answered, "I don't know." ¹³ They brought the man who was initially blind to the Pharisees. ¹⁴ It was on the Sabbath when Jesus made mud and healed the

John 9

man. ¹⁵ The Pharisees also asked how the man received his sight. So the man said, "He put mud over my eyes, then I washed it off, and I could see." ¹⁶ Some of the Pharisees said, "This man is not from God, for he works on the Sabbath." But others said, "How can a sinner make miracles?" And there was division among them. ¹⁷ They turned to the man who was formerly blind and said, "What will you say about him, the one who opened your eyes?" He answered, "He is a prophet."

¹⁸ The Jewish leaders did not believe that he was initially blind, so they summoned his parents. ¹⁹ They asked them, "Is this your son, the one you say was born blind? How is it that he can see?" ²⁰ His parents answered, "We know this is our son and that he was born blind. ²¹ What we don't know is how he can see, or who healed him. Ask him, he is old enough to speak for himself." ²² His parents said this because they feared the Jews, who declared that anyone who confessed that Jesus is the Christ would be removed from the synagogue. ²³ That's why his parents said, "He is old enough. Ask him."

²⁴ For the second time they called the man who was formerly blind and said, "Give glory to God. We know that this man called Jesus is a sinner." ²⁵ He said, "I don't know whether he is a sin-

ner, but I do know that I was blind and, now I can see." ²⁶ They asked him, "What did he do to you, and how did he open your eyes?" ²⁷ He answered, "I already told you, and you did not listen. Why do you want to hear it again? Do you also want to become his disciples?" ²⁸ They denounced him and said, "You are his disciple, but we are disciples of Moses. ²⁹ We know God spoke to Moses, but we don't know where this man comes from."

³⁰ The man said, "Isn't that amazing? You don't know where he is from, and he was the one who healed my eyes. ³¹ We know that God doesn't listen to sinners, but he will hear anyone who worships him and does his will. ³² Ever since the world began, it was unheard of a man opening the eyes of a person born blind. ³³ This man could make no miracle if he was not from God," ³⁴ so they responded, "You were born completely in sin and you dare teach us? Then they cast him out.

³⁵ Jesus heard that they threw the man out, and he found him and said, "Do you believe in the Son of Man?" ³⁶ The man asked, "Who is he, Lord, that I may believe in him." ³⁷ Jesus said, "You have seen him, and he is the one speaking with you." ³⁸ The man said, "Lord, I believe." And he worshipped him. ³⁹ Then Jesus told him, "For judgment I entered the world, so that the blind may

John 9

see and those who think they see will become blind." **⁴⁰** Some Pharisees were nearby, and they heard his words and said, "Are we also blind?" **⁴¹** Jesus said, "You would not be guilty if you were blind. But you think you can see, so your sin remains."

¹ "Truly and certainly, whoever does not enter the sheepfold by the gate, but climbs in another way is a thief and robber. ² The one who enters through the gate is the shepherd of the flock. ³ The doorkeeper opens the gate for him, and the sheep hear his voice. He calls his own sheep by name and leads them out. ⁴ After bringing them all outside, he walks ahead of them, and the sheep follow him because they know his voice. ⁵ They won't follow a stranger, but will flee from him, because they don't recognize the stranger's voice." ⁶ Jesus gave them this illustration, but they did not understand what he meant.

⁷ Then he said, "Truly I say to you, I am the gate for the sheep. ⁸ All who came before me were thieves and robbers, but the sheep chose not to hear them. ⁹ I am the gate, and those who come through me will be saved. They will go in and out, and find pasture. ¹⁰ The thief comes only to steal, kill, and destroy. I have come so they may life and have it abundantly. ¹¹ I am the good shepherd, and the good shepherd lays down his life the sheep. ¹² The hired man is not the shepherd and does not own the sheep. He will abandon them and run away when he sees a wolf coming, so the wolf attacks the flock and scatters them. ¹³ The man flees because he is a hired worker, and he does not care about the sheep. ¹⁴ I am the good shep-

John 10

herd. I know my sheep, and they know me. ¹⁵ Just as the Father knows me, and I know him, I lay down my life for the sheep. ¹⁶ I have other sheep that are not from this fold, and I must bring them too. They shall hear my voice, and there will be one flock with one shepherd. ¹⁷ The Father loves me because I give up my life, so that I may take it up again. ¹⁸ No one can take it from me, but I lay it down on my own. I have the right to give it up, and I have the power to take it again. For this is what my Father commanded."

¹⁹ The people were divided again because of these words. ²⁰ Many of the Jews said, "He has a demon and he has lost his mind." ²¹ Others replied, "These are not the words of a man under demonic possession. Can a demon open the eyes of the blind?" ²² It was now winter, and the Festival of Dedication took place in Jerusalem. ²³ Several boats from Tiberias landed near the place where they had eaten the bread after the Lord had given thanks. ²⁴ Then the people surrounded him and asked, "How long will you keep us in suspense? If you are the Messiah, tell us plainly." ²⁵ Jesus replied, "I have told you, and you don't believe. The works that I do in my Father's name testify about me, ²⁶ but you won't believe me because you are not my sheep. ²⁷ My sheep hears my voice; I know them, and they follow me. ²⁸ I

give them eternal life, and they will never die. No one can snatch them out of my hand. ²⁹ My Father, who has given them to me, is greater than all. No one can take them out of his hand. ³⁰ I am one with the Father."

³¹ Again the people picked up rocks to stone him. ³² Jesus said, "I have done many good works from the Father. For which work are you stoning me for?" ³³ They responded, "We are not stoning you for a good work, but for blasphemy. You are a man who claims to be God."

³⁴ Jesus replied, "Is it not written in your Law that God said to certain men, 'I say, you are gods'? ³⁵ Those people who were called gods received God's word, and the Scripture cannot be changed. ³⁶ So are you saying to the one whom the Father set apart and sent into the world, that he is blaspheming because I said that I am God's son? ³⁷ If I don't do my Father's works then don't believe me. ³⁸ But if I do his works and you don't believe me, then believe the works. Then you will know and understand that the Father is in me, and I am in the Father."

³⁹ Again they tried to arrest him, but he escaped. ⁴⁰ Jesus went across the Jordan River and stayed in the place where John first baptized. ⁴¹ Many people came to him and said, "John made no miracles, but everything he said about this man was

true." ⁴² Many in that place believed in Jesus.

John 11

¹ Now a man named Lazarus was sick, and he lived in Bethany with his sisters: Mary and Martha. ² Mary was the one who anointed the Lord's feet with oil and wiped it with her hair, whose brother Lazarus was sick. ³ The sisters sent a message to Jesus, "Lord, the one you love is sick." ⁴ When Jesus heard it, he said, "This sickness will not result in death, but for the glory of God, so the Son of God will be glorified by this. ⁵ Jesus loved the three of them, ⁶ and he heard that Lazarus was sick, before he stayed where he was for the next two days.

⁷ Then he said to his disciples, "Let's go back to Judea." ⁸ But his disciples replied, "Rabbi, the Jews tried to stone you, and you are going there again?" ⁹ Jesus answered, "Aren't there twelve hours in a day? Anyone who walks in daytime will not stumble, because he sees the light of this world. ¹⁰ But whoevers walks in the night will stumble, because there is no light." ¹¹ Then he said, "Our friend Lazarus is only asleep, but I will go and wake him up." ¹² The disciples replied, "Lord, he will recover if he is sleeping." ¹³ Jesus meant that he was dead, but they thought he said that he was asleep. ¹⁴ Then Jesus clearly said, "Lazarus is dead. ¹⁵ I am glad for your sakes that I was not there, so you may believe. Let us go to him." ¹⁶ Then Thomas the one called Twin said

John 11

to his fellow disciples, "Let us also go so we may die with him."

[17] When Jesus arrived, he heard that Lazarus was in the tomb for four days. [18] Bethany was less than two miles away from Jerusalem, [19] and many of the Jews came to comfort Martha and Mary in the loss of their brother. [20] When Martha heard that Jesus was coming, she went out to meet him, while Mary stayed at home. [21] Martha said to Jesus, "Lord, my brother would not be dead if you were here sooner. [22] But even now I believe God will grant you whatever you ask of him."

[23] Jesus said, "Your brother will rise again." [24] Martha replied, "I know he will rise in the resurrection at the last day. [25] Jesus answered, "I am the resurrection and the life. Whoever believes in me will live, even after death. [26] Everyone who lives and believes in me shall never die. Do you believe this?" [27] Martha said, "Yes, Lord. I believe you are the Messiah, the Son of God who comes into the world." [28] After saying this, she returned to Mary and told her in private, "The Teacher is here and is asking for you." [29] Then Mary got up at once to see him.

[30] Jesus had not yet entered the town, but was in the place where Martha met him. [31] The people who consoled Mary in the house saw her

get up and leave hastily. They followed her, and assumed she was going to weep at the tomb. ³² When Mary arrived and saw Jesus, she fell at his feet and said, "Lord, my brother would not have died if you were here sooner." ³³ Jesus saw her weeping with people who joined her, and he was angry in the spirit and deeply troubled. ³⁴ He said, "Where have you put him?" They answered, "Lord, come and see." ³⁵ So Jesus wept, ³⁶ and the people said, "See how much he loved him!" ³⁷ But some of them said, "He healed a blind man, so couldn't he have saved Lazarus from death?"

³⁸ Jesus groaned in the spirit, and came to the tomb. It was a cave with a stone that sealed the entrance. ³⁹ He said, "Remove the stone," and Martha replied, "Lord, he reeks of decay, and it has been four days." ⁴⁰ Jesus answered, "Have I not said that if you believe, you would see God's glory?" ⁴¹ So they removed the stone, and he looked up and said, "Father, thank you for hearing me. ⁴² I know you always hear me, but I said it out loud for the people standing here, so they will believe that you sent me." ⁴³ Jesus shouted, "Lazarus, come out!" ⁴⁴ The dead man came out, his hands and feet were bound with linen strips, and his face was wrapped in cloth. Jesus said to them, "Unwrap him and let him go." ⁴⁵ Then many of those who came to Mary saw this miracle and

John 11

believed in him. ⁴⁶ But some of them went to the Pharisees to report what Jesus did.

⁴⁷ The chief priests and the Pharisees gathered the Sanhedrin council, and said, "What will we do since this man is making many miracles? ⁴⁸ If we let him be then everyone will believe in him, and the Romans will come and remove both our temple and nation." ⁴⁹ Caiaphas, the high priest at the time, said, "You know nothing at all. ⁵⁰ Don't you realize that it is better for you that one man die for the people than for the whole nation to be destroyed?" ⁵¹ He did not say this on his own, but being high priest that year he prophesied that Jesus would soon die for the nation. ⁵² And not just for the nation, but also to unite the scattered children of God. ⁵³ So from that day onward, they plotted to kill him.

⁵⁴ Then Jesus stopped going openly among the Jews, and he went to a place near the wilderness to a town called Ephraim, where he stayed with his disciples. ⁵⁵ The Jewish Passover was near, and many travelled from the country to Jerusalem for purification before the Passover. ⁵⁶ They searched for Jesus in the temple zone and asked each other, "What do you think? He won't come to the festival, will he?" ⁵⁷ The chief priests and the Pharisees gave orders that anyone who sees him must report it, so he could be arrested.

John 12

¹ Six days before the Passover, Jesus came to Bethany where Lazarus lived, and raised him from the dead. ² They made him dinner, and Martha was serving, when Lazarus was among those who joined him at the table. ³ Then Mary took a pound of aromatic oil and anointed Jesus' feet then wiped his feet with her hair; the entire house was filled with the fragrant scent.

⁴ Judas Iscariot, the disciple who would betray him, said, ⁵ "Why wasn't that fragrant oil sold for three hundred denarii and given to the poor?" ⁶ He said it because he was a thief who steals while serving as treasurer of the disciples, and he did not care for the poor. ⁷ Jesus replied, "Leave her alone. She kept this for the day of my burial. ⁸ You will always have the poor with you, but you won't always have me."

⁹ Many people knew that Jesus was there and they came not for him, but to see Lazarus, whom he raised from the dead. ¹⁰ Then the chief priests decided to kill Lazarus too ¹¹ because many of the Jews had deserted them and believed in Jesus. ¹² The next day the big crowd that had come to the festival heard that Jesus would arrive in Jerusalem. ¹³ They took palm branches and went to out to meet him. They shouted, "Hosanna! Blessed is he who comes in the name of the Lord! Blessed is the king of Israel!" ¹⁴ Jesus

John 12

sat on the young donkey that he found, as it is written, ¹⁵ "Fear not, daughter Jerusalem. Look, your king is coming, seated on a donkey's colt. ¹⁶ His disciples did not understand this at first. But after he was glorified, they remembered that this was written about him and this was done to him.

¹⁷ The crowd that was with him when Lazarus was called out of the tomb, and raised from death was proclaiming the word. ¹⁸ This led to people meeting him because they heard of the miracle. ¹⁹ Then the Pharisees said to one another, "Be aware, that we have achieved nothing. Look, everyone is following him!"

²⁰ Some Greeks were among those who went to worship at the festival. ²¹ They came to meet Philip, who was from Bethsaida in Galilee. They said, "Sir, we want to see Jesus." ²² Philip told Andrew, and they went together to tell Jesus.

²³ Jesus said, "The hour has come for the Son of Man to be glorified. ²⁴ Truly and certainly, unless a grain of wheat falls in the ground and dies, it remains alone. But if it dies, it bears much fruit. ²⁵ Whoever loves his life will lose it, and those who hate their life in this world will secure it for eternity. ²⁶ Whoever serves me must follow me, because my servant must be where I am. My Father will honour those who serve me. ²⁷ Now my soul is troubled. What can I pray, Father,

save me from this hour? But this is the reason why I came. ²⁸ Father, bring glory to your name." Then a voice came from heaven and said, "I have brought glory to my name, and I will do it again." ²⁹ The people that stood nearby heard the voice, and said it was thunder. Others said that an angel had spoken to him.

³⁰ Jesus said, "The voice came for your benefit, not mine. ³¹ Now is the time for judgment of this world. Now the ruler of this world will be cast out. ³² And I will draw all people to myself, when I am lifted up from the earth." ³³ He said this to tell how he was going to die. ³⁴ The crowd responded, "We have heard from the Scripture that the Messiah will live forever. How can you say the Son of Man must be lifted up? Who is this Son of Man?"

³⁵ Jesus answered, "The light will be with you for a little longer. Walk while you have the light so the darkness won't overtake you. The one who walks darkness doesn't know where he is going. ³⁶ While you have the light, believe in it so you may become children of the light." Jesus said this before leaving, and he stayed hidden from them.

³⁷ They still did not believe him after he had made many miracles. ³⁸ This was to fulfill the word of Isaiah the prophet, who said, "Lord,

John 12

who has believed our message? And who did the Lord reveal his arm to?" ³⁹ The people could not believe, for Isaiah had said, ⁴⁰ "He blinded their eyes and hardened their hearts so they can neither see with their eyes, or understand with their hearts and be converted, and I would heal them."

⁴¹ Isaiah said this because he saw God's glory and spoke of him. ⁴² Still, many believed in him including the rulers, but they did not confess because of the Pharisees so that they would not be banned from the synagogue. ⁴³ They loved human praise more than the praises from God.

⁴⁴ Jesus shouted, "Whoever believes in me believes not only in me, but also in God who sent me. ⁴⁵ The one who sees me also sees the one who sent me. ⁴⁶ I have come as light into the world, so everyone who believes in me will not remain in darkness. ⁴⁷ I have come to save the world and not to judge it, so I will not condemn those who hear my words, but disobey. ⁴⁸ The one who rejects me along with my word shall be judged on the last day by the truth that I have spoken. ⁴⁹ I do not speak on my own, but the Father who sent me, commanded me what I should say and how to say it. ⁵⁰ I know that his command leads to eternal life. So I say what the Father tells me to say."

John 13

¹ Before the Passover Festival, Jesus knew that his hour had come to leave this world and return to the Father, having loved his own who were in the world, he loved them to the end. ² By suppertime, the devil had already prompted Judas, Simon Iscariot's son, to betray him. ³ Jesus knew that the Father had given everything into his hands and that he had come from God and would return to him. ⁴ So he got up from the table, took off his robe, and wrapped a towel around his waist. ⁵ Then he poured water into a basin and started to wash his disciples' feet, drying them with the towel that was wrapped around him.

⁶ He came to Simon Peter, who said, "Lord, are you going to wash my feet?" ⁷ Jesus answered, "You don't understand what I am doing now, but later you will." ⁸ Peter said, "No, you will never wash my feet!" Jesus replied, "You will have no part with me unless I wash you." ⁹ Peter said, "Lord, wash not only my feet, but also my hands and my head." ¹⁰ Jesus replied, "Those who had a bath do not need to wash, except for the feet, to be fully clean. You are clean, but not all of you." ¹¹ For he knew who would betray him, which is why he said, "You are not all clean."

¹² After washing their feet, he put on his robe and sat at the table. He said, "Do you know what I have done for you? ¹³ You call me Teacher

John 13

and Lord – you spoke correctly, because I am. ¹⁴ Not that I, your Lord and Teacher, have washed your feet, you ought to wash each other's feet. ¹⁵ I gave you an example to follow, so do as I have done to you. ¹⁶ Truly and certainly, the servant is not greater than his master, and the messenger is not greater than the one who sent him. ¹⁷ If you know these things, you are blessed for doing them.

¹⁸ I know those I have chosen and I am not speaking about each of you. But this fulfills the Scripture: the one who eats my bread has turned against me. ¹⁹ I tell you this in advance, so when it happens you will believe that I am God's Son. ²⁰ Truly and certainly, whoever accepts my messenger accepts me, and whoever welcomes me welcomes the one who sent me."

²¹ When Jesus had said this, he was troubled in spirit and testified, "Truly I say to you, one of you will betray me." ²² The disciples looked at each other uncertain of whom he meant, ²³ and the disciple that Jesus loved, was seated next to him at the table. ²⁴ Simon Peter motioned to him to ask whom Jesus spoke of, ²⁵ so the disciple leaned over to Jesus and asked, "Lord, who is it?" ²⁶ Jesus answered, "The one I give the bread to when it is dipped." He dipped the bread and gave it to Judas, Simon Iscariot's son. ²⁷ Satan en-

tered into Judas when he ate the bread, and Jesus said to him, "What you are doing, do it quickly." ²⁸ None of the others at the table knew what he meant. ²⁹ Since Judas was their treasurer, some of them thought Jesus told him to buy provisions for the festival, or to give something to the poor. ³⁰ Judas left at once after taking the bread, and it was night.

³¹ When Judas was gone, Jesus said, "Now the Son of Man will be glorified, and God will be glorified through him. ³² If God is glorified in him, then he will give glory to the Son and he will do it at once. ³³ Children, I am with you a little longer. And as I have said to the Jews, you will search for me, but you cannot come to where I am going. ³⁴ So here is a new command: love one another. Just as I have loved you, you must also love each other. ³⁵ By this everyone shall know that you are my disciples, if you have love for one another."

³⁶ Simon Peter asked, "Where are you going, Lord?" Jesus answered, "You can't follow me now to my destination, but you will follow me later." ³⁷ Peter said, "Lord, why can't I follow you now? I will lay down my life for you." ³⁸ Jesus replied, "Will you lay down your life for me? Truly and certainly, a rooster will not crow until you have denied me three times."

John 14

¹ "Don't let your hearts be troubled. Trust in God, and believe in me. ² There are my rooms in my Father's house. If it were not so, I would have told you that I am leaving to prepare a place for you. ³ And if I leave prepare a place for you, I will return to bring you to me, so that you will be where I am. ⁴ You know the way to where I will go." ⁵ Thomas said, "Lord, we don't know where you will go, so how can we know the way?" ⁶ Jesus said, "I am the way, the truth, and the life. No one comes to the Father except through me, ⁷ and if you really know me you would know who my Father is. From now on, you know him and you have seen him. ⁸ Philip said, "Lord, show us the Father and it will be enough for us."

⁹ Jesus replied, "Have I been with you all this time and you still don't know me, Philip? Whoever has seen me has seen the Father. How can you say, 'Show us the Father'? ¹⁰ Don't you believe that I am in the Father and the Father is in me? The words I say to you are not my own; but the Father who dwells in me does his works. ¹¹ Believe that I am in the Father, and the Father is in me. Or trust me because of my miracles. ¹² Truly and certainly, whoever believes in me will do the works that I have done. And he will do greater works than these, because I am going to the Father. ¹³ What you ask for in my name, I will

do it so the Father may be glorified in the Son. ¹⁴ Ask for anything in my name, and I will do it. ¹⁵ If you love me then keep my commands. ¹⁶ I will ask the Father, and he will give you another comforter to be with you forever. ¹⁷ He is the Spirit of Truth, and the world can't receive him since it doesn't see him or know him. But you know him, because he lives with you and will be in you.

¹⁸ I won't leave you as orphans; I will come to you. ¹⁹ Soon the world will no longer see me, but you will see me. Because I live, you will live also. ²⁰ On that day you will know that I am in my Father, you are in me, and I in you. ²¹ Those who accept my commands and keep them are the ones who love me. Those who love me shall be loved by my Father, and I will love them and reveal myself to them."

²² The other Judas, not Iscariot, said, "Lord, how is that you are going to reveal yourself to us, and not to the world?" ²³ Jesus said, "Whoever loves me will keep my word. My Father will love them, and we will come and make our home with them. ²⁴ Whoever doesn't love me won't keep my words. The word that you hear is not mine but is from the Father who sent me. ²⁵ I have told you these things while I remain with you. ²⁶ But the Counselor, the Holy Spirit, whom the Father will send in my name, will teach you all things and

John 14

remind you of all that I have said to you.

²⁷ Peace I leave with you. My peace I give unto you. I don't give to you, as the world gives so don't let your heart be troubled or afraid. ²⁸ Remember what I said, I am going away and coming back to you. If you love me, you would rejoice that I am going to the Father, because he is greater than I. ²⁹ I have told you now before it happens so when it does happen, you will believe. ³⁰ I won't speak with you much longer, because the ruler of this world is coming. He has no power over me. ³¹ The world will know that I love the Father and I do what he requires of me. Get up and let's be going.

¹ "I am the true vine, and my Father is the gardener ² who cuts off every branch of mine that bears no fruit, and he trims the branches that do bear fruit so they will be more productive. ³ You are now clean because of the word I have given you. ⁴ Remain in me, and I will remain in you. No branch can bear fruit by itself unless it remains on the vine; you cannot be fruitful unless you remain in me. ⁵ I am the vine and you are the branches. The one who remains in me and I in him will produce much fruit, because you can do nothing apart from me.

⁶ Whoever does not remain in me is discarded like a branch that withers. Such branches are gathered into a pile to be burned. ⁷ If you remain in me and my words remain in you, ask for whatever you desire and it will be granted. ⁸ My Father is glorified when you produce much fruit, proving that you are my disciples. ⁹ As the Father has loved me, I have also loved you. Abide in my love. ¹⁰ If you keep my commands, you will abide in my love, just as I have kept my Father's commands and I abide in his love. ¹¹ I have told you these things so that my joy may be found in you and your joy may be complete.

¹² Here is my command: love each other as I have loved you. ¹³ There is no greater love than

John 15

to lay down one's life for his friends. ¹⁴ You are my friends if you obey my command. ¹⁵ I won't call you bondservants anymore, because a master does not confide in them. You are now my friends because I have told you everything that the Father told me. ¹⁶ You did not choose me, but I chose you. I appointed you to go and produce lasting fruit so that whatever you ask of the Father in my name, will be granted. ¹⁷ Here is my command: love each other.

¹⁸ If the world hates you, remember it hated me first. ¹⁹ The world would love you as its own if you belonged to it, but you don't belong to the world. I have chosen you to come out of the world, so the world hates you. ²⁰ Remember what I said, 'A slave is not greater than his master.' They persecuted me, so they will persecute you also. If they listened to my word, they would listen to yours also. ²¹ They will do these things to you because of my name, since they don't know the One who sent me. ²² They would not be guilty if I had not come and spoken to them, but now they have no excuse for their sin. ²³ Whoever hates me hates my Father too. ²⁴ If I made no miracles among them that no one else could do, they would not be guilty. But they have seen my works, and they hate both me and my Father." ²⁵ This fulfills what was written in their scripture:

they hated me for no reason. ²⁶ I will send you the Comforter, the Spirit of truth who will proceed from the Father and he will testify about me. ²⁷ You will also testify, for you have been with me from the beginning.

John 16

¹ I have told you these things to save you from falling away. ² They will cast you out of the synagogue. Even so, a time is coming when whoever kills you will think he is doing a service to God. ³ They will do these things because they have never known the Father or me. ⁴ I am telling you this now so when it happens, you will remember my warning. I did not tell you this from the beginning because I was with you.

⁵ But now I will return to the one who sent me, and none of you ask where I am going. ⁶ Rather, your hearts are filled with grief because of what I said. ⁷ Even so, it is best for you that I go away, since the Comforter won't come if I don't leave; but if I go, I will send him to you. ⁸ When he comes, he shall convict the world of sin, righteousness, and judgment. ⁹ Of sin, because they don't believe in me. ¹⁰ Of righteousness, because I am going to the Father and you will no longer see me. ¹¹ Of judgment, because the ruler of this world has been judged.

¹² There is much more for me to tell you, but you can't bear it now. ¹³ When the Spirit of truth comes, he will guide you into all truth. He will not talk on his own, but he shall speak what he hears, and tell you about the future. ¹⁴ He will bring me glory, because he will receive from me and declare it to you. ¹⁵ Everything the Father has

is mine. That's why I said the Spirit receives from me and declares it to you. ¹⁶ Soon you will no longer see me, then soon after you'll see me again."

¹⁷ Some of his disciples asked each other, "What does he mean when he says, 'Soon you will no longer see me, then soon after you'll see me,' and 'I am going to the Father'? ¹⁸ What does he mean by 'soon? We don't know what he is talking about." ¹⁹ Jesus knew they wanted to ask him, so he said, "Are you asking yourselves what I meant? I said, 'Soon you will no longer see me then soon after you'll see me again.' ²⁰ Truly I say to you, you will weep and mourn, but the world will rejoice. You will grieve, but your sorrow will transform into joy. ²¹ A woman in labor has pain when her time is due; but when her child is born, her suffering turns to joy because she has brought a baby into the world. ²² So you have sorrow now, but I will see you again; then your hearts will rejoice, and no one can rob you of that joy.

²³ On that day you won't ask me for anything. Truly and certainly, whatever you ask the Father in my name shall be granted. ²⁴ Until now you requested for nothing in my name. Ask and you will receive so your joy may be complete.

²⁵ I have spoken of these things to you in rhetoric, and a time is coming when I will stop speaking to you in this manner; I will tell you

John 16

plainly about the Father. ²⁶ On that day you will ask in my name. I am not saying that I will ask the Father on your behalf. ²⁷ The Father himself loves you because you have loved me and believed that I came from God. ²⁸ I came from the Father and entered the world. Now I am leaving the world to return to the Father."

²⁹ His disciples said, "Now you are speaking clearly without rhetoric. ³⁰ Now we know that you know everything and don't need anyone to question you, so we believe you came from God." ³¹ Jesus said, "Do you now believe? ³² Behold, the hour is coming and it has arrived, when each of you will be scattered to your own home, and you will leave me alone. Yet I am not alone because the Father is with me. ³³ I have told you these things so that in me you will have peace. You will have many struggles in the world, but be strong. I have overcome the world."

¹ After Jesus said this, he looked up to heaven and said, "Father, the hour has come. Glorify your Son, so that the Son may glorify you. ² For you have given him authority over all people, so he may give eternal life to all you have given him. ³ This is eternal life: for them to know you, the only true God, and Jesus Christ whom you have sent. ⁴ I brought you glory on the earth by completing the work you gave me to do. ⁵ Now, Father, glorify me in your presence with the glory we shared before the world began.

⁶ I have revealed you to the ones you gave me from the world. They were yours, you gave them to me, and they have kept your word. ⁷ Now they know everything I have is a gift from you. ⁸ For I have given them the words you have given me, which they received and certainly know that I came from you. They believe that you sent me. ⁹ I pray for them, but I don't pray for the world except the ones you have given me, because they are yours. ¹⁰ Everything I have is yours, and everything you have is mine. I have been glorified in them. ¹¹ I am leaving the world, and they will stay behind. I am coming to you. Holy Father, protect them in your name, the name you gave me, that they will be one as we are one. ¹² I protected them by the power of your name you have given me, and kept them safe when I was with

John 17

them. Not one is lost except the one headed for destruction so Scripture would be fulfilled.

¹³ Now I am coming to you, and I speak these things in the world so they will have my joy fulfilled in them. ¹⁴ I have given them your word, and the world hates them since they don't belong it, as I am not of the world. ¹⁵ I'm not asking you to remove them from the world, but to keep them from the evil one. ¹⁶ They don't belong to the world, as I am not of the world. ¹⁷ Sanctify them by the truth. Your word is truth. ¹⁸ As you sent me into the world, I am sending them into the world. ¹⁹ I sanctify myself for them so they may also be sanctified by the truth.

²⁰ I pray not only for them, but also for those who will believe me through their message. ²¹ May they all become one, as you, Father, are in me and I am in you. May they also be one in us so the world may believe that you sent me. ²² I gave them the glory that you gave me, so they may be one as we are one. ²³ I am in them and you are in me. May they be made perfect in one, so the world may know that you have sent me and have loved them as you have loved me. ²⁴ Father, I want those you have given me to be with me where I am. Then they will see the glory that you have given me because you loved me before the world began. ²⁵ Righteous Father, the world

doesn't know you, but I do. My disciples know that you sent me. ²⁶ I have revealed your name to them and will make it known, so your love for me will be in them, and I will be in them."

John 18

¹ After speaking those words, Jesus and his disciples went across the Kidron Valley, where there was a garden and they entered it. ² Judas, who betrayed him, also knew the place, because Jesus had often gone there with his disciples. ³ The chief priests and Pharisees gave Judas a group of soldiers and temple guards to accompany him to the garden. They came with lanterns, torches and weapons. ⁴ Jesus knew everything that would happen to him, so he went out and said, "Who are you looking for?"

⁵ They answered, "Jesus of Nazareth." Jesus said, "I am he," and Judas the betrayer stood with them. ⁶ When Jesus said, "I am he," they stepped back and fell to the ground. ⁷ Then he asked them again, "Who are you looking for?" They said, "Jesus of Nazareth." ⁸ Jesus replied, "I told you that am he. If you came for me, then let these men go." ⁹ This happened to fulfill the words he had said, "I have not lost any of those you have given me."

¹⁰ Then Simon Peter drew his sword and cut off the right ear of Malchus, the high priest's slave. ¹¹ Jesus told Peter, "Sheathed your sword. Will I not drink the cup the Father has given me?" ¹² Then the soldiers, their commander and the Jewish officers arrested Jesus and bound him. ¹³ First they took him to Annas, for he was the father in law of Caiaphas, the high priest that year.

¹⁴ It was Caiaphas who told the Jews that it was better for one man to die for the people.

¹⁵ Simon Peter and another disciple followed Jesus. The high priest knew that disciple, so he let him enter his courtyard with Jesus. ¹⁶ Peter had to wait outside the gate, and the disciple who knew high priest, spoke to the woman by the gate, and she let Peter in. ¹⁷ The woman said to Peter, "You're not one of this man's disciples, are you?" He replied, "I am not." ¹⁸ The servants and officers made a fire because it was cold, and they stood there warming themselves, and so did Peter.

¹⁹ The high priest questioned Jesus inside about his disciples and what he taught them. ²⁰ Jesus said, "I have preached openly to the world; I have always taught in the synagogue and in the temple where everyone gathers, and I haven't said a word in secret. ²¹ Why do you question me? Ask those who heard me. They know what I said." ²² Then one of the temple guards standing nearby slapped Jesus in the face and said, "Is this the way to answer the high priest." ²³ Jesus replied, "If I said something wrong then prove it. But I have spoken correctly, so why did you hit me?" ²⁴ Then Annas sent him bound to the high priest.

²⁵ Now Simon Peter stood there and

John 18

warmed himself. They said to him, "You aren't one of his disciples too, are you?" He denied it and said, "I am not." ²⁶ One of the high priest's slaves, a relative of the man whose ear Peter cut off, said, "Didn't I see you with him in the garden?" ²⁷ Peter denied it again, and the rooster crowed at once. ²⁸ Then they took Jesus from Caiaphas to the governor's estate at dawn, and his accusers stayed outside to avoid defilement, so they could eat the Passover meal.

²⁹ Pilate came out to them and said, "What charges have you brought against him?" ³⁰ They replied, "We wouldn't have brought him to you if he were not a criminal." ³¹ Pilate said, "Take him away and judge him by your own law." The Jews replied, "The Law forbids us to kill anyone." ³² This fulfilled what Jesus said about how he would die. ³³ Pilate went back inside the governor's estate and summoned Jesus, and asked, "Are you the king of the Jews?"

³⁴ Jesus said, "Is this your own question, or have others told you about me?" ³⁵ Pilate answered, "Am I Jew? Your own nation and chief priests delivered you to me. What have you done?" ³⁶ Jesus replied, "My kingdom is not of this world, and if it were, my followers would fight to prevent my arrest by the Jews. But my kingdom is not of this world." ³⁷ Pilate said, "So you are a

king?" Jesus replied, "You say that I am a king. I was born to enter the world and to testify to the truth. Everyone who accepts the truth hears my voice."

⁳⁸ Pilate asked, "What is truth? Then he went out to the Jews and said, "There are no grounds for charging him. ³⁹ You have a custom of asking me to release one prisoner at the Passover. Do you want me to release the King of the Jews?" ⁴⁰ They shouted back, "Not this man! Release Barabbas!" They freed Barabbas the rebel.

John 19

¹ Then Pilate had Jesus beaten with a whip. ² The soldiers wove a crown of thorns and put it on his head, and made him wear a purple robe. ³ They lined up and said, "Hail, King of the Jews!" Then slapped his face. ⁴ Pilate went outside again and said to the Jews, "I'm bringing him out to you, so you will know that I have no grounds to convict him. ⁵ Then Jesus came out wearing the crown of thorns and purple robe. Pilate said to them, "Here is the man!"

⁶ When the chief priests and officers saw him, they shouted, "Crucify him! Crucify him!" ⁷ The Jews replied, "We have a law, and according to this law he must die, because he claimed to be God's son." ⁸ When Pilate heard this, he became more afraid. ⁹ He went back inside the estate and asked Jesus, "Where are you from?" But Jesus gave no answer. ¹⁰ Pilate said, "Why aren't you speaking to me? Don't you know that I have power to release you, or to crucify you?"

¹¹ Jesus answered, "You would have no power over me at all, if it weren't given to you from above. So the one who handed me over to you has the greater sin." ¹² Then Pilate tried to release him, but the Jews shouted, "If you release this man, you are not Caesar's friend. Anyone who makes himself a king opposes Caesar." ¹³ When Pilate heard this, he brought Jesus outside

and sat on the judgment seat in a place called the Stone Pavement, or Gabbatha in Hebrew.

¹⁴ It was about the sixth hour on the day of preparation for the Passover. Pilate told the Jews, "Here is your king!" ¹⁵ They shouted, "Take him away! Take him away! Crucify him!" Pilate said, "Should I crucify your king?" The chief priests answered, "We have no king but Caesar." ¹⁶ Then Pilate handed him over to be crucified, and the soldiers took Jesus away.

¹⁷ Carrying his own cross, he went to Golgotha, Hebrew for place of a Skull. ¹⁸ There they crucified him and two others beside him, with Jesus in between. ¹⁹ Pilate posted a sign on the cross that read, "Jesus of Nazareth, the King of the Jews." ²⁰ The place where Jesus was crucified was near the city, and many people read the sign that was written in Hebrew, Latin, and Greek. ²¹ Then the chief priests said to Pilate, "Change it from 'The King of the Jews,' to 'He said, I am King of the Jews.'" ²² Pilate responded, "What I have written I have written."

²³ When the soldiers crucified Jesus, they took his clothes and divided them equally among the four of them. They also took his seamless robe that was woven in one piece from top to bottom. ²⁴ They told themselves, "Let's not tear it, but cast lots to see who will get it." This ful-

John 19

filled the Scripture that said, "They divided my clothes among themselves, and cast lots for my garment." That was what the soldiers did.

^{25} By the cross of Jesus stood his mother, her sister, Mary the wife of Clopas, and Mary Magdalene. ^{26} When Jesus saw his mother standing beside the disciple he loved, he said to her, "Woman, here is your son." ^{27} Then he said to his disciple, "Here is your mother," and from then on the disciple took her into his home. ^{28} Jesus knew that everything was now accomplished, and to fulfill Scripture he said, "I am thirsty."

^{29} A jar of sour wine was nearby, and they soaked a sponge in it, placed it on a hyssop branch, and held it up to his mouth. ^{30} When Jesus had sipped the wine, he said, "It is finished." Then he bowed his head and gave up his spirit.

^{31} It was the day of preparation, and the Jews did not want the bodies to remain on the cross on the Sabbath, for this particular Sabbath was special. They asked Pilate to break the men's legs and take the bodies away. ^{32} Then the soldiers came and broke the legs of the two men who were crucified with Jesus. ^{33} When they came to Jesus, and saw that he was already dead, they did not break his legs. ^{34} But a soldier pierced his side with a spear, and at once blood and water came out. ^{35} The one who saw this has testified, and his word is true. He speaks the truth so that you may also believe. ³⁶ These things happened to fulfill the Scriptures, "Not one of his bones will be broken, ³⁷ and "They will look at the one they pierced."

³⁸ Afterward, Joseph of Arimathea, the secret disciple of Jesus who feared the Jews, asked Pilate for permission to take down Jesus' body. Pilate allowed it, so he came and took the body away. ³⁹ Nicodemus, who came to Jesus earlier at night, joined him and brought a seventy-five pounds mixture of myrrh and aloes. ⁴⁰ Then they took Jesus's body and wrapped it in linen cloths with spices, according to the Jewish burial customs. ⁴¹ The place where Jesus was crucified had a garden, and in the garden was a tomb, which was never used. ⁴² They put Jesus there since the tomb was nearby on the Jewish day of preparation.

John 20

¹ Early on Sunday morning, when it was still dark, Mary Magdalene came to the tomb and saw that the stone had been removed from the entrance. ² She ran to Simon Peter and the other disciple, whom Jesus loved, and said, "They have taken the Lord out of tomb, and we don't know where they put him." ³ So Peter and the other disciple departed for the tomb.

⁴ They were both running, and John outran Peter and reached the tomb first. ⁵ He stooped down and saw the linen cloths lying there, but did not go in. ⁶ Then Simon Peter arrived and went inside. He also noticed the linen cloths lying there, ⁷ and the cloth that covered Jesus' head was folded up and lying apart from the other wrappings. ⁸ Then the other disciple, who outran Peter, entered the tomb and saw, and believed. ⁹ They still did not understand the Scripture that said Jesus must rise from the dead, ¹⁰ so they went home.

¹¹ Mary stood outside the tomb crying, and as she wept, she stooped and looked inside. ¹² She saw two angels in white that sat there, one at the head and one at the feet, where the body of Jesus had lain. ¹³ The angels said, "Woman, why are you crying?" She replied, "Because they have taken away my Lord, and I don't know where they have put him." ¹⁴ Then she turned around

and saw Jesus standing there, but did not recognize him.

¹⁵ Jesus said, "Woman, why are you crying? Who are you looking for?" She thought he was the gardener and said, "Sir, if you have carried him away, tell me where you have put him, and I will get him." ¹⁶ Jesus said, "Mary." Turning around, she said to him in Hebrew, "Rabboni!" Which means Teacher. ¹⁷ Jesus said, "Don't cling to me, for I have not yet ascended to the Father. Go and tell my brothers that I am ascending to my Father and your father; to my God and your God."

¹⁸ Mary Magdalene came and told the disciples, "I saw the Lord," before telling what he said to her. ¹⁹ That Sunday evening the disciples met behind closed doors because they feared the Jews. Then Jesus came and stood among them, and said, "Peace be to you." ²⁰ He showed them his hands and side, and they rejoiced when they saw the Lord. ²¹ Again he said, "Peace be to you. As the Father has sent me, I am sending you." ²² He breathed on them and said, "Receive the Holy Spirit." ²³ If you forgive anyone's sins, they are forgiven, but if you don't forgive them, they aren't forgiven."

²⁴ One of the twelve, Thomas *the twin* was not with them when Jesus came. ²⁵ So they said,

John 20

"We have seen the Lord." But he replied, "I won't believe unless I see the nail marks in his hands, and put my finger into those nailed wounds, and put my hand into his side.

²⁶ The disciples met again after eight days, and Thomas was with them. Even when the doors were locked, Jesus appeared and stood among them. He said, "Peace be with you." ²⁷ Then he said to Thomas, "Put your finger here, and see my hands. Put your hand into my side, and don't doubt, but believe." ²⁸ Thomas said, "My Lord and my God!" ²⁹ Jesus replied, "You believe because you have seen me. Blessed are those who believe without seeing."

³⁰ Jesus made many other miracles before his disciples, which are not recorded in this book. ³¹ But these are written so that you may believe Jesus is the Messiah, the Son of God, and by believing you will have life in his name.

John 21

¹ Later, Jesus appeared again to his disciples by the Sea of Galilee. This is how it happened. ² Simon Peter, Thomas *the twin*, Nathanael from Cana in Galilee, the sons of Zebedee, and two other disciples were together. ³ Simon Peter said, "I'm going fishing," and they said, "We're coming too." So they went out in the boat, but they caught nothing all night.

⁴ At dawn, Jesus stood on the shore, but the disciples couldn't see who he was. ⁵ He called to them, "Fellows, have you caught any fish?" They said, "No." ⁶ Then he said, "Cast the net on the right side of the boat, and you'll find some." So they did, and there were so many fish that they couldn't haul in the net.

⁷ The disciple whom Jesus loved said to Peter, "It's the Lord!" After hearing that, Simon Peter wrapped his coat around him, for he was stripped for work, and plunged into the water. ⁸ The other disciples came in the boat and towed the net full of fish, for they were only about a hundred yards from the shore. ⁹ When they got there, they saw a charcoal fire with fish on top, and bread. ¹⁰ Jesus said, "Bring some of the fish that you just caught." ¹¹ Simon Peter got up and dragged the net to shore: there were one hundred fifty-three large fish and the net wasn't torn. ¹² Jesus said, "Come and have breakfast." None of

John 21

the disciples dared to ask him, "Who are you? For they knew it was the Lord. ¹³ Jesus came, took the bread, and gave it to them then served them fish. ¹⁴ This was third time that Jesus appeared to his disciples since he was raised from the dead.

¹⁵ After breakfast, Jesus asked Simon Peter, "Simon, son of John, do you love me more than these?" Peter answered, "Yes, Lord. You know that I love you." Jesus said, "Feed my lambs."

¹⁶ Again Jesus said, "Simon, son of John, do you love me?" Peter said, "You know that I love you." Jesus said, "Take care of my sheep."

¹⁷ The third time Jesus said, "Simon, son of John, do you love me?" Peter was hurt that Jesus asked him the question a third time. He replied, "Lord, you know everything. You know that I love you?" Jesus said, "Feed my sheep."

¹⁸ Truly and certainly, when you were young, you would tie your belt and walk wherever you wanted. But when you are old, you will stretch out your hands and someone else will tie you, and carry you where you don't want to go." ¹⁹ He said this to tell how Peter would die and glorify God. Then Jesus said, "Follow me."

²⁰ Peter turned around and saw the disciple whom Jesus loved following them. He was the one who leant over to Jesus at the supper and asked, "Lord, who will betray you?" ²¹ Peter saw

him, and said to Jesus, "Lord, what about him?" ²² Jesus said, "If I want him to remain until I come, what is that to you? You have to follow me."

²³ So the rumor spread among the believers that John wouldn't die. Jesus did not say that he wouldn't die, but only said, "If I want him to remain until I come, what is that to you?"

²⁴ This disciple is the one who testifies to these events and has recorded them here. We know that his testimony is true, ²⁵ and Jesus did many other things too, and if they were all written down, I suppose the world couldn't contain the books that would be written.

Sin created a rift between God and mankind. Jesus died on the cross, rose to life and became our link to God. He came to reconcile men with God so that you could make peace with him today.

You can pray by saying, "Jesus died for me and I repent of my sins. I believe and receive him as the Lord and redeemer. Amen."

www.ingramcontent.com/pod-product-compliance
Lightning Source LLC
Chambersburg PA
CBHW051410290426
44108CB00015B/2230